Football

Marshall Cavendish
Benchmark

This edition first published in 2010 in North America by Marshall Cavendish Benchmark

Marshall Cavendish Benchmark
99 White Plains Road
Tarrytown, NY 10591
www.marshallcavendish.us

Published in 2009 by Evans Publishing Ltd, 2A Portman Mansions, Chiltern St, London WIU 6NR

Editor: Nicola Edwards
Designer: D.R. Ink
All photographs by Wishlist except for: p6 Jeff Gross/Getty Images; p7 Al Bello/Getty Images;
p8 G. Newman Lowrance/Getty Images; p9 Ronald Martinez/Getty Images; p10 Jonathan Daniel/
Getty Images; p11 Charles Eshelman/FilmMagic; p13 Tom Hauck/Getty Images; p14 Scott Boehm/
Getty Images; p27 Jonathan Daniel/Getty Images; p28 Jim McIsaac/Getty Images

Library of Congress Cataloging-in-Publication Data

Gifford, Clive.
 Football / by Clive Gifford.
    p. cm. — (Tell me about sports)
 Includes bibliographical references and index.
 Summary: "An introduction to football, including techniques, rules, and the training regimen of
 professional athletes in the sport"—Provided by publisher.
 ISBN 978-0-7614-4456-5
 1. Football—United States—Juvenile literature. I. Title.
 GV950.7.G535 2009
 796.332—dc22

                                    2009004828

Printed in China.
135642

Contents

Tell Me About...
Football

▲

Larry Fitzgerald makes a spectacular catch to score a touchdown for the Arizona Cardinals in 2009. The Cardinals beat the Atlanta Falcons 30–24.

Football is an action-packed, high-impact team sport. It mixes physical play with **strategy,** or plays that are planned and practiced before games. Each team plays both offense and defense during a game.

The two teams in a game try to move the ball up the field into the opposing team's **end zone** to score points. Teams can throw or run with the ball to score a **touchdown** or kick the ball through the goal posts to score a **field goal**. The team with the higher score at the end of the game wins!

A football game is made up of four 15-minute-long quarters. There is a break at halftime after the second quarter. In the National Football League (NFL), if the score is tied at the end of the fourth quarter, a 15-minute period of overtime is played.

Teams are allowed to take time-outs during a game. The clock also stops when the ball goes out of bounds and when a player is injured, which means that a game can last three or four hours.

Although each team is only allowed to have eleven players on the field at one time, many football teams have more than forty players. This is because players have specialized roles and are split into offense, defense, and special teams. The job of the offense is to score. The defense prevents the other team from scoring. Special teams handle kicking plays.

An offensive team gets four **downs**, or chances, to move the ball at least 10 yards (9.1 meters) forward. If the team succeeds, it has made a first down and gets four more chances to move another 10 yards. If they fail, the ball is handed to the opposing team.

▲ Tackles are often rough in professional football. Here, Clinton Portis of the Washington Redskins is driven back by two members of the New York Giants.

▼ The quarterback is the player who makes most of the passes when playing offense. Here, he has spotted that one of his receivers is open and throws a forward pass.

Touchdowns and Scoring

The goal of the offense is to score a touchdown, which is worth six points. To score a touchdown, a player must either carry the ball into the end zone or catch it in the end zone.

After a successful touchdown, the team that has scored gets a chance to earn an extra point. The ball is given to the kicker who tries to kick the ball through the two goal posts at the back of the end zone to score a one-point conversion. Sometimes a team will decide to try

▼ The Arizona Cardinals' Tim Hightower dives into the end zone to score a touchdown against the Kansas City Chiefs.

◀ This receiver outruns his opponent and carries the ball into the end zone to score a touchdown.

for a two-point conversion. From the 3-yard line, the team tries to pass or run the ball into the end zone for a second time.

There are two other ways of scoring points. A field goal, worth three points, is scored when the kicker kicks the ball through the goal posts. Teams can attempt a field goal from anywhere on the field on any down, but they are usually done on the fourth down and inside the 45-yard line. The defensive team can score two points when it traps opponents with the ball in their own end zone. This is called a safety and is an uncommon play.

▼ Morten Anderson kicks the conversion for the Atlanta Falcons that made him the all-time leading scorer in 2006.

Football Stars

The NFL regular season starts at the beginning of September and runs into January, when postseason play-off games begin. The Super Bowl, the NFL's championship game, is usually played on the first Sunday in February.

▼ NFL training camps involve lots of hard work. Here a player practices his blocking using a blocking sled at the Green Bay Packers 2007 training camp.

The Most Valuable Players

Quarterback Joe Montana is the only player to win three Super Bowl Most Valuable Player (MVP) awards.

In Super Bowl XLII in 2008, the New York Giants quarterback Eli Manning was the MVP. The year before, the MVP was awarded to the Indianapolis Colts quarterback—Eli's brother, Peyton!

▲ Peyton (*left*) and Eli Manning both throw a ball at a special event for NFL fans held in New York City. Top NFL stars are expected to help promote the sport.

Before the season starts NFL teams hold training camps. Coaches get their players ready for the season and practice strategies. They also use training camp to trim the team roster, or list, to fifty-three players. Players must perform well in training to stay on the team.

During the regular season each of the 32 NFL teams plays 16 games. The top 12 teams enter a series of play-off games. A team must win all its play-off games to make it to the Super Bowl.

Top NFL players are paid well, but they must train incredibly hard, work out in the gym, and be careful about what they eat.

Football is a rough contact sport and many players get injured. Sometimes injuries cause a player to sit out for the rest of the season. A very bad injury can end a player's career in the NFL.

Equipment and the Field

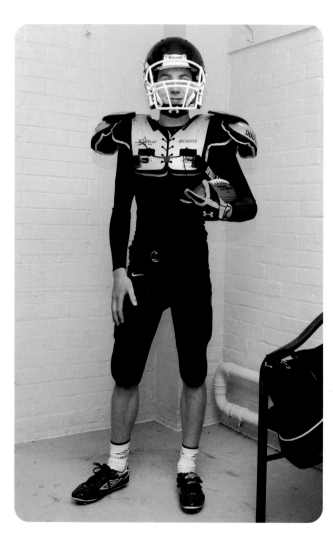

▲ Players suit up in their team's locker room before the game. This player has on his shoulder pads, helmet, and padded pants. He will wear his jersey over his protective gear.

Since tackling and forceful collisions are a regular part of football, players wear a lot of protective gear to reduce the chance of injury.

Football players wear thigh, knee, rib, and elbow pads, as well as an athletic supporter to protect the groin. A helmet has a face mask, a mouth guard, and a chin guard. All players also wear shoulder pads, which are different depending on a player's position. For example, quarterbacks, who throw the ball, may wear a lighter set of shoulder pads than linebackers, who tackle frequently.

A football field is 100 yards (91.4 m) long and 53 yards (48.5 m) wide. There is a 10-yard (9 m) end zone that begins at each goal line. At the back of each end zone are the goal posts. Lines run across the field every 5 yards (4.6 m). Every other 5-yard line has a number showing the distance in yards to the nearest end zone. The 50-yard line runs across the middle of the playing field.

◄

The player with the ball has run over the sideline and is out of bounds. The next play, taken from the nearest hash mark, will restart the game. The player must have control of the ball before going out of bounds.

A Football Field

Hash marks every yard (0.91 m) up the field.

Goal posts (uprights)

Sideline

End zone

End line

50-yard halfway line

Goal line

The Line of Scrimmage

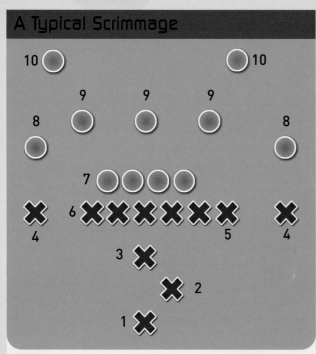

A Typical Scrimmage

10   10
9   9   9
8   8
7
6
4   5   4
3
2
1

Offense		Defense
1. Running back	4. Wide receiver	7. Defensive line
2. Full back	5. Tight end	8. Cornerback
3. Quarterback	6. Offensive line	9. Linebacker
		10. Safety

Every game starts with a kickoff. The team that will begin playing defense kicks the ball down the field to the other team, the offense, who then runs it as far back up the field as possible. Play begins from wherever the returner is tackled.

Each down begins with the teams lining up at the **line of scrimmage**. This is where the officials rule the ball should be to start the next down.

The offense, the team in possession of the ball, can line up in different ways. Usually, this includes a line of five offensive linemen. Their job is to protect the quarterback and clear the path for receivers. The offensive lineman playing center starts each down with a **snap**, usually to the quarterback. Other offensive players include the wide receiver, the tight end, and the running backs—the halfback, tailback, and full back.

▶ The officials who measure whether a team has gained enough distance for a first down are called the chain crew.

▲ An offensive lineman in a three-point stance (*left*) and a defensive back in a four-point stance face each other just before the play begins.

Once the play begins, the defense aims to get past the offensive linemen and either tackle the quarterback before he passes or tackle the running back who has the ball. The defensive line tries to occupy the offensive linemen. This allows the linebackers to rush the quarterback and enables the cornerbacks and safeties to cover the receivers.

If the ball lands out of bounds or touches the ground before anyone catches it, then the pass is ruled incomplete and the line of scrimmage doesn't change. If a receiver or running back moves the ball forward, the next down begins from where that player was tackled or forced out of bounds.

▼ This center uses a shotgun, or long, snap to pass the ball 4 to 5 yards (3.5 or 4.5 m) back to the quarterback. This gives him extra time and space to play.

The Quarterback

The quarterback is the team's leader during offensive play. The coach signals plays to him from the sidelines and then he tells the players before they line up so

▲ Throwing a ball well takes lots of practice. The thrower steps forward, turning his hips and shoulders to face the target. He flicks his wrist as he releases the ball to help it spin and travel smoothly toward its target.

everyone knows what to do once the ball is snapped. A quarterback may change the play in the last seconds before the snap. This is called an audible.

Once the quarterback has the ball, he can then make one of three types of plays. He may hand the ball to a running back, throw the ball to a receiver, or run with the ball himself. When throwing the ball, the quarterback flicks his wrist to make the ball spin so that it moves faster and is more accurate. This is called a spiral.

Quarterbacks expect protection from their team's offensive linemen. If opponents break through the line and if the quarterback still has the ball, the defense may **sack**, or tackle, him.

▲ This quarterback is handing the ball to a running back who will sprint and squeeze his way through a gap in the defensive line.

▼ When throwing a football, your fingers should be spread with your little finger on the middle of the laces and your index finger near the back of the ball.

Quarterbacks

Quarterbacks are often the highest-paid players on an NFL team. In 2008, Ben Roethlisberger signed a contract with the Pittsburgh Steelers worth $102 million over eight years!

Brett Favre holds many NFL quarterback records, including most touchdown passes (454), most passes completed (5,464), and most starts in a row for a quarterback, an amazing 257.

In the NFL, quarterbacks and defensive players have microphones and speakers inside their helmets so that they can be in radio contact with their coaches.

Receiving and Running

To complete a pass, teams need both good quarterbacks and skilled receivers. Receivers should be fast to outrun defenders and should be able to catch the ball while on the move. They must keep their eyes on the ball until it is in their hands. It is also important that they bring their hands into their body as they catch the ball so that it won't bounce out or get knocked free by a defender.

Receivers don't want to **fumble** the ball, otherwise the other team may gain possession. They also try to run away from the defense to avoid an **interception**.

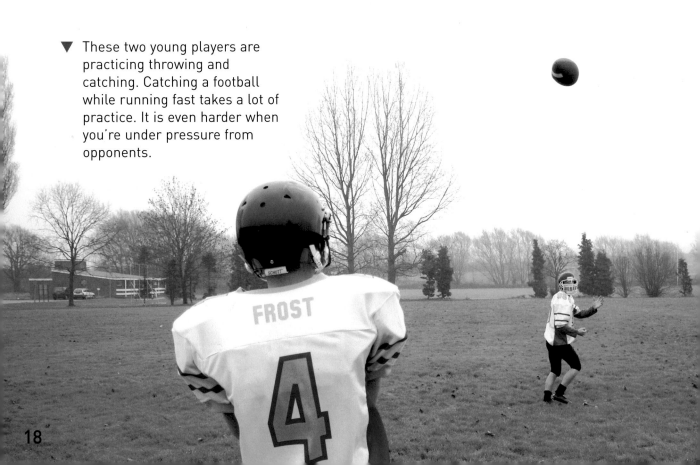

▼ These two young players are practicing throwing and catching. Catching a football while running fast takes a lot of practice. It is even harder when you're under pressure from opponents.

Interceptions can often lead to a touchdown for the other team. This is because the offensive team is not in a good position to defend the end zone and stop the runner.

Sometimes, teams use complicated plays to outwit the defense so the receiver will be open for a pass. Once a receiver has the ball, he or she will sprint hard toward the end zone, swerving to avoid the defense.

Long passes can be risky, so sometimes a team will use a running play in which the quarterback hands the ball to a running back. The running back then tries to burst through gaps in the defensive line created by the other offensive players. Receivers help block on these plays.

▼ This receiver is sprinting hard. He holds the ball in one hand, cradled in between the side of his body and his elbow. His free hand can be used to fend off opponents.

▼ This wide receiver has outsprinted the defense and leaps high to catch a pass.

Tackling and Blocking

Stopping the other team from scoring or gaining a first down is very important for the defending team. Defensive players try to tackle the player with the ball as quickly as possible so the offense doesn't advance far toward the end zone.

Defensive players must time their tackles carefully. They can cause a pass interference **penalty** if they tackle receivers before they have caught the ball. In the NFL, this penalty means the line of scrimmage is moved up to where the pass would have been caught.

▼ Tacklers tend to aim for the waist, driving their shoulder into the other player's stomach and wrapping their arms around him to stop him.

▲ These linemen (*right, in white shirts*) are blocking, keeping their opponents at bay long enough for their quarterback to make a good pass.

Before the officials signal a down, tacklers are allowed to try to wrestle the ball out of their opponent's hands. This may occur when a second tackler arrives to help.

Blocking is a crucial skill when on offense. Players must keep defenders away from a teammate with the ball. Blocking attempts occur at every scrimmage when the offensive linemen try to keep defenders away from the quarterback. Blocking can also create gaps for a running back to run through with the ball or for a receiver to catch the ball.

Blockers can use their hands and arms to push defenders away but must not hold onto them or tackle them. Blocks cannot be made from behind or below the waist, otherwise the offense will get a penalty.

Special Teams

When kicking or returning a kick is needed, it's time to call up special teams. These players—the kicker, the punter, the long snapper, and the returner—may only be on the field for a few moments of each game, but they can make the difference between a win or a loss.

▲ This player makes a long punt. See how high his kicking foot follows through. This helps the ball travel farther.

The kicker starts every game by kicking off, sending the ball deep into the other team's territory. A kickoff is also used to restart the game after a team has scored, and to start the second half. The kicker and the long snapper come out for field goal attempts and for one-point conversions.

▲
A teammate holds the ball in position with his fingers. The kicker backs up and then runs toward the ball to kick it.

▲
This punt returner has gained possession of the ball and is running forward. He aims to gain as much territory as possible before he is tackled.

Teams often choose to **punt** when they are on their fourth down and are not close to making a first down. The punter stands 10 yards (9 m) or more behind the line of scrimmage. He must catch the ball, step forward, and drop-kick the ball smoothly and quickly. His teammates will chase the punt and try to tackle the opponent with the ball as quickly as possible.

When a team is receiving a kickoff or a punt, it will also bring out special-team players. This will include a returner who catches the ball and returns it up the field as far as possible.

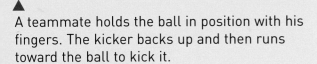

▼ To score a field goal, players need to work together. The center snaps the ball back to the holder who catches it and places it in position for the kicker.

Flag Football

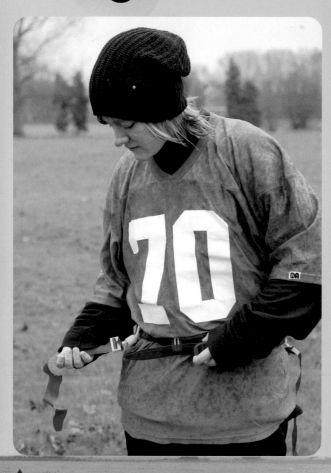

Many people play versions of football where there is less contact and no need to wear a helmet and lots of padding. One of the most popular is flag football. It is a good way for both boys and girls to get started in football and learn some of the basic skills.

Flag football players wear little to no padding. They do wear one or two pieces of material called flags that are often attached to a belt. Removing a flag from the player with the ball is equal to tackling in full-contact football.

▲
A player adjusts her belt and holds one of the flags that are attached to the side.

When a flag is removed, the down is over. The next down will start from where the flag was removed. Whether you are playing defense or offense, you will need to be sharp and react quickly to opponents to make or avoid a "tackle."

According to the U.S. Flag Football Association (USFFA) rules, each team should have eight players on the field. The game is played on a field 80 yards (73 m) long. Contact blocking is allowed between the waist and shoulders, but holding is not allowed.

▲ The player with the ball is about to lose her flag. Once it has been removed from the belt, she is tackled and the play is over.

▼ The quarterback (*left*) waits for the snap as the teams face off at the line of scrimmage.

The World of Football

The NFL may be the top football league, but there are dozens of other competitions both in North America and around the world. Many of these follow rules slightly different from those of the NFL.

College football is very popular in the United States. Games between top-ranked teams sell out 100,000-seat stadiums. Many college football players go on to play in the NFL, which holds its draft each spring.

There are women's football leagues in America, as well, including the Independent Women's Football League and the National Women's Football Association.

▼ Miaya Tolbert, playing for the Detroit Demolition, is tackled by two members of the Chicago Force. This Independent Women's Football League game ended with Detroit winning 19–0.

▲ New York Dragons' Chin Achebe (45) scores a touchdown against the Dallas Desperados. This Arena Football League game was played indoors at New York's Nassau Coliseum.

Although the sport started in the United States, it is popular elsewhere, too. The German Football League, Japan's X-League, and the British American Football League (BAFL) are just a few. In 1999 the International Federation of American Football (IFAF) began holding world cup competitions. Countries from all over the world now compete.

In Competition

In the very first game the United States played in the 2007 World Cup, they beat South Korea 77–0!

The London Olympians are the most successful BritBowl team. They have played in the BritBowl eleven times and have won nine championship titles.

In 1916, a college game between the Cumberland Bulldogs and Georgia Tech Engineers entered the record books. Georgia Tech won by an incredible score . . . 222–0!

Where Next?

These websites and books will help you to find out more about football.

Websites
http://www.nflrush.com
NFL Rush is an official NFL website designed specifically for younger fans. It contains videos of game action, information on star players, and lots of fun activities.

http://www.sikids.com/football/nf
Sports Illustrated's website for kids has a section that covers the NFL, including game schedules, statistics, and news.

http://www.ncaa.com
The National College Athletics Association has a website dedicated to college football teams that includes news, standings, and information on each team.

http://www.arenafootball.com
The official site of the Arena Football League with information on the teams, players, and schedules. There is also a great explanation of the rules of arena football.

Books
Buckley, James Jr. *Eyewitness: Football*. New York: DK Children, 1999.

Kennedy, Mike. *Football*. New York: Children's Press, 2002.

Football Words

down The period of action that starts when the offense puts the ball in play and ends when the officials rule the play is over.

end zone The 10-yard (9.1 m) section at each end of a football field where touchdowns are scored.

field goal A play worth three points made by kicking the ball through the goal posts.

fumble To lose hold of a football while running with it or handling it.

interception When a pass by one team is caught by a player on the other team.

line of scrimmage The place on the field where a play begins.

penalty A punishment given by the referees to a team that breaks the game rules.

punt A kick made when a player drops the ball and kicks it downfield to move the other team back.

sack When the quarterback is tackled behind the line of scrimmage.

snap When a center passes the ball between his legs to a teammate standing behind him to begin a down.

strategy A planned play.

touchdown A six-point score made by running or catching the ball in the end zone.

Index

Numbers in **bold** refer to pictures.